be strong

Compiled by Dan Zadra & Kristel Wills
Designed by Jessica Phoenix & Sarah Forster
Created by Kobi Yamada

COMPENDIUM™
INCORPORATED

live inspired.

ACKNOWLEDGEMENTS

These quotations were gathered lovingly but unscientifically over several years and/or were contributed by many friends or acquaintances. Some arrived—and survived in our files—on scraps of paper and may therefore be imperfectly worded or attributed. To the authors, contributors and original sources, our thanks, and where appropriate, our apologies. –The Editors

WITH SPECIAL THANKS TO

Jason Aldrich, Gerry Baird, Jay Baird, Neil Beaton, Josie Bissett, Laura Boro, Melissa Carlson, M.H. Clark, Tiffany Parente Connors, Jim & Alyssa Darragh & Family, Rob Estes, Pamela Farrington, Michael & Leianne Flynn & Family, Dan Harrill, Michael J. Hedge, Liz Heinlein & Family, Renee Holmes, Jennifer Hurwitz, Heidi Jones, Sheila Kamuda, Michelle Kim, Carol Anne Kennedy, June Martin, David Miller, Carin Moore & Family, Moose Josh Oakley, Tom DesLongchamp, Steve & Janet Potter & Family, Joanna Price, Heidi & José Rodriguez, Diane Roger, Alie Satterlee, Kirsten & Garrett Sessions, Andrea Shirley, Jason Starling, Brien Thompson, Helen Tsao, Anne Whiting, Heidi Yamada & Family, Justi & Tote Yamada & Family, Bob & Val Yamada, Kaz & Kristin Yamada & Family, Tai & Joy Yamada, Anne Zadra, August & Arline Zadra, and Gus & Rosie Zadra.

CREDITS

Compiled by Dan Zadra & Kristel Wills
Designed by Jessica Phoenix & Sarah Forster
Created by Kobi Yamada

ISBN: 978-1-932319-58-3

3rd Printing.   Printed in China

The best thing to hold onto
in life is each other.

~ Audrey Hepburn ~

You are never alone. Sooner or later, tough times come to us all, and you'll quickly realize that you are not alone—your friends and family are here, too.

Hope can open the door to change, so surround yourself with people who share your hopes. Faith can move mountains, so surround yourself with people who believe you can and will prevail. Love can do anything, so surround yourself with people who love and care for you.

Vincent van Gogh once wrote, "People must believe in each other, and feel that it can be done and must be done; in that way they are enormously strong." The truth is, there are no problems so big that we cannot solve them together. We are always bigger than anything that can happen to us.

The human spirit is stronger than
anything that can happen to it.

~ George C. Scott ~

The bravest sight in all the world is
someone fighting against the odds.

~ Franklin Lane ~

Doubt whom you will,
but never yourself.

~ Christine Bovee ~

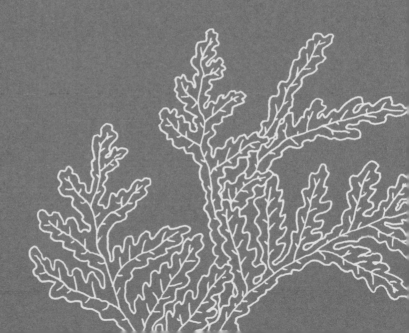

Do just once what others say you cannot do, and you will never pay attention to their limitations again.

~ Edmund Brown, Jr. ~

If you're strong enough,
there are no precedents.

~ F. Scott Fitzgerald ~

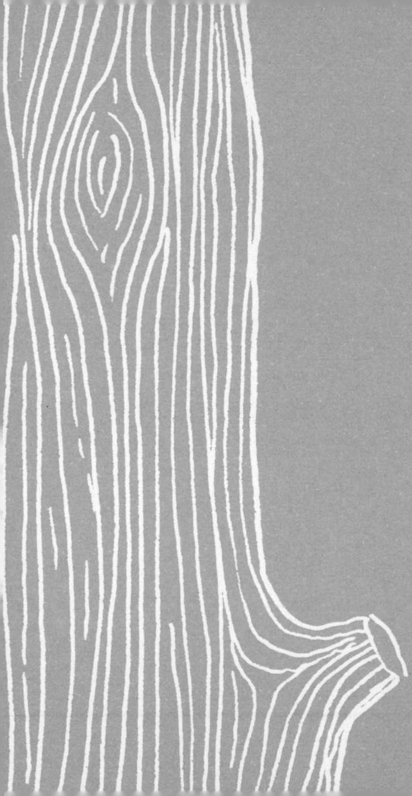

Refuse to accept the many reasons
why it can't be done and ask if there
are any reasons that it can be done.

~ Hanoch McCarty ~

We are never powerless.

~ Jane Seymour ~

No matter what the statistics say,
there's always a way.

~ Bernie Siegel ~

Although the world is full of suffering,

it is also full of the overcoming of it.

~ Helen Keller ~

Someday all you'll have
to light the way will be
a single ray of hope—
and that will be enough.

~ Kobi Yamada ~

I haven't a clue how my story will end,
but that's all right. When you set out on
a journey and night covers the road,
that's when you discover the stars.

~ Nancy Willard ~

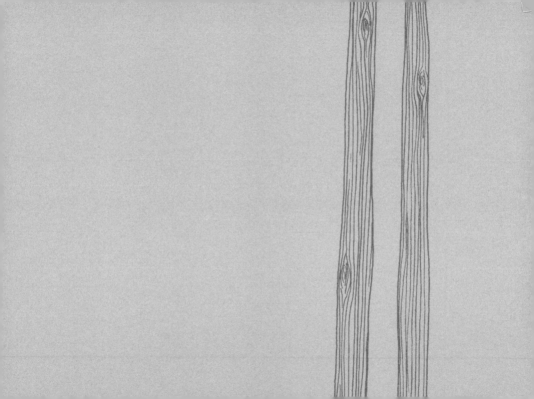

The best work is done with the
heart breaking, or overflowing.

~ Mignon McLaughlin ~

Laughter in the face of reality is one of the finest sounds there is. In fact a good time to laugh is any time there is.

~ Linda Ellerbee ~

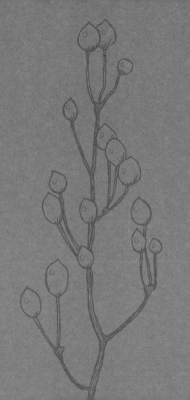

Wherever there's a shadow
there's a light.

~ Edgar Linton ~

Tonight when you lay your head on your pillow, forget how far you still have to go. Look instead at how far you've already come.

~ Bob Moawad ~

Standing your ground is progress
when you're battling a hurricane.

~ David Weinbaum ~

Difficulties are meant to rouse,
not discourage.

~ William Ellery Channing ~

You may have to fight a battle
more than once to win it.

~ Margaret Thatcher ~

When you get into a tight place, and everything goes against you till it seems as if you couldn't hold on a minute longer, *never give up then*, for that's just the place and time that the tide'll turn.

~ Harriet Beecher Stowe ~

For all your troubles I give you laughter.

~ François Rabelais ~

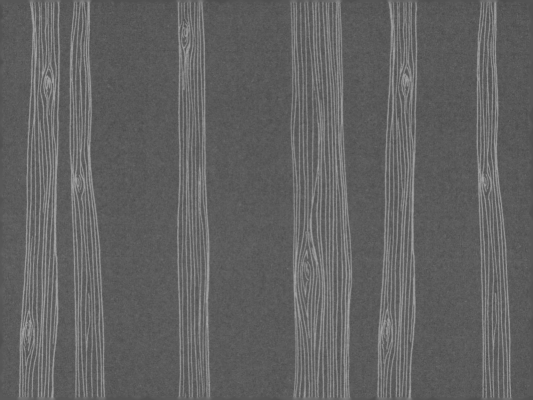

The best way out
is always through.

~ Robert Frost ~

You got yourself this far—
you just got to keep going.

~ Don Ward ~

Nothing lasts forever...not even your troubles.

~ Arnold Glasgow ~

I will persist. I will always take another step. If that is of no avail I will take another, and yet another.

~ Og Mandino ~

We define ourselves by
the best that is in us,

not the worst that has
been done to us.

~ Edward Lewis ~

I am not a victim. I am a survivor.

~ Lance Armstrong ~

Perhaps I am stronger than I think.

~ Thomas Merton ~

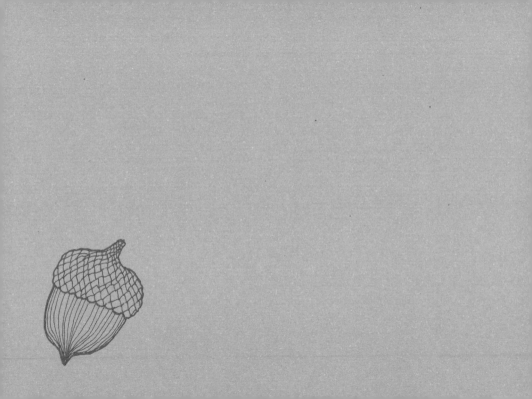

We acquire the strength of that
which we have overcome.

~ Ralph Waldo Emerson ~

Surround yourself with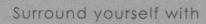

people who believe you can.

~ Dan Zadra ~

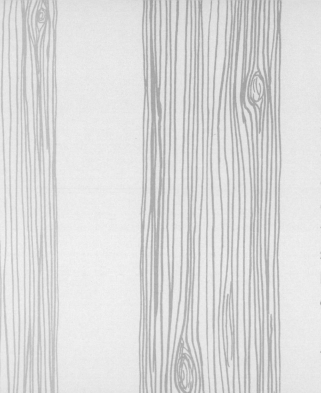

People must believe
in each other, and
feel that it can be
done and must be
done; in that way
they are enormously
strong. We must
keep up each
other's courage.

~ Vincent van Gogh ~

Friendship glows in the dark.

~ Cat Lane ~

Trouble is a part of life, and if you don't share it you don't give the person who loves you a chance to love you enough.

~ Dinah Shore ~

Lend me your hope for awhile. A time will come when I will heal, and I will lend my renewed hope to others.

~ Eloise Cole ~

Courage comes and goes.
Hold on for the next supply.

~ Thomas Merton ~

Hang in there. It is astonishing how short a time it can take for very wonderful things to happen.

~ Frances H. Burnett ~

Just for today I will be happy. Just for today I will try to live through this day only, not to tackle my whole life problem at once. I can do things for twelve hours that would appall me if I had to keep them up for a lifetime. Just for today...

~ Sybyl F. Partridge ~

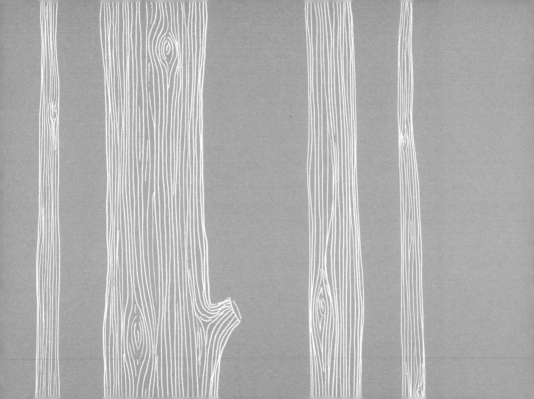

Today I live in the quiet, joyous
expectation of good.

~ Ernest Holmen ~

Just remember—when you think
all is lost, the future remains.

~ Bob Goddard ~